Kaleidoscope

PERSPECTIVES ON LIFE, FAITH, AND COUNTRY

Phyllis,

the book!

Enjoy

Leo Wicker

Kaleidoscope

PERSPECTIVES ON LIFE, FAITH, AND COUNTRY

Colors of Life and Faith in America

Les C. Wicker

NAPLES, FLORIDA

2018

> Mailing Address:
> 9520 Ironstone Terrace #202
> Naples, FL 34120
>
> Email: leswicker@aol.com

Ordering Information:

This book is available from Amazon.com. For bulk purchas-
es, please contact the author.

Book Layout ©2018 BookDesignTemplates.com
Interior and cover design by Araby Greene
Cover photo © Fyria – Shutterstock

Kaleidoscope: Perspectives on Life, Faith, and Country /
Les C. Wicker —1st ed.

Printed in the United States of America

ISBN: 978-1-7270-5204-6 (pbk.)

Contents

Preface vii

The Colors of Growth in Your Personal Life 9

You Can Be a Border Buster 9

Do Good Anyway 12

Things That Offend 14

God and Golf 17

The Ten Commandments of Marriage 19

The Colors of Growth and Development in Your
Community of Faith 23

Marketing Your Church 23

To Grow or Not to Grow 28

The Changing Landscape of Church Life 35

Pastor Assassinators Are All Too Familiar 36

Double Standard for Clergy 39

Healthy Churches Manage Pastoral Relations 41

Who Governs the Church? 44

Protocol in Addressing Your Pastor 47

Applause in Church 48

Sunday Morning Competition 50

The Colors of Patriotism and Polarization in America 53

The Land of the Free and the Home of the Brave 53

Who Were the Pilgrims 57

Thanksgiving: A Distinctly American Holiday 59

Reconciling America 61

Some Gave Some—Some Gave All 63

Freedom Is Never Free 64

Attack Ads and the 9th Commandment 66

The Politics of Negativity 67

Freedom "From Religion" and the Miniscule
    Minority 69

Why Shouldn't Students Say "God Bless
    America!" 72

The Prince of Peace and the Angst of the Day 76

A More Excellent Way 78

Overwhelmed by Sadness 79

Appropriate Racial Identification 81

The War on Christmas 83

The Colors of Holidays and Seasons 85

Saint Valentine's Day 85

The Silent Spring No More, But Who Is Listening ... 87

The Four Facets of Mother's Day 89

Ten Commandments for Father's Day 91

Memorial Day: Truly a Religious Holiday 93

Labor Day Is Far More Than the End of Summer 95

World Communion Sunday—A Paradigm for Faith
    Communities 97

Why I Love Thanksgiving 99

The "Get Ready" People 101

Santa Vs Jesus 102

Final Thoughts 104

About the Author 107

Preface

A kaleidoscope is an optical instrument with reflecting surfaces tilted to each other at an angle so that one or more parts on one end mirrors the objects or colors on the other end in a symmetrical pattern when viewed from the opposite end, due to repeated reflection. The reflectors or mirrors are normally enclosed in a tube often containing colored pieces of glass or some transparent material to be reflected into the viewed pattern. Rotating the cell containing the transparent material will cause motion of the materials which will result in an ever-changing color dynamic. Kaleidoscope is the proper designation for this book as the barrel of perspective is in constant change.

This book is a kaleidoscope of thoughts about personal growth, the ever-changing dynamic of religious life and church development, perspectives and challenges of patriotism in America, and finally reinvigorating the meaning of some special holidays that have lost their meaning. The book may be read as a whole or read chapter by chapter as each chapter stands alone.

Readers who have an interest in growing their personal lives may focus on Chapter I which centers around becoming the person one wishes to become and challenges to negativity. Readers who have a special interest in issues surrounding religious life, church growth, and clergy, will find perspectives in Chapter II. Issue oriented readers in terms of political life, patriotism, angst in the country, and ways to address such concerns will find Chapter III addressing many present-day topics. Finally, the changing dynamic of a number of holidays has left the original purpose of those special days in the shadows. Remembering why they were formed and designated brings a renewed sense of appreciation for why they exist and what meanings can be attached to them.

Enjoy this kaleidoscope. May it bring perspective, challenge, and insight, to significant concerns for your life, faith, and country.

Les C. Wicker

CHAPTER 1

The Colors of Growth in Your Personal Life

You Can Be a Border Buster

How many people, some well-meaning family members or friends, have advised you to "stay put." Staying put means staying in your comfort zone where life is easy and there are no particular challenges.

It is ever so easy to heed the advice of these well-intentioned people as you know they do not want you to take risks that may bring you hurt in some way, such as a much sought-after dream that never materializes. Yes, but! There is a yearning in your heart to reach beyond yourself and to have your life fulfilled with all you were created to be. Should you go for your dream?

Often the people who want you to stay put have a vested interest in your staying put. They do not want to lose you from their close circle as you are a source of comfort and companionship. Having you around fortifies their life in certain ways. They gain something because you are there for them. You become a source of affirmation for who they are. You fulfill their needs. They may further be threatened in the sense of having been left behind if you leave your comfort zone along with them and cross a border for a greater dream. It is often in their interests to tell you to stay where you are. They may even offer some persuasive arguments as to why it is better to stay where you are than to follow your dream.

But there are others who will not only grant you the freedom to seek your dream, but will encourage you to do so. They will be waving you on, giving you "the okay," "the go-for-it," because they want your life to be fulfilled so that you can be all you were created to be. While these people may be in their comfort zone, more likely than not, they have already crossed a border to a dream fulfilled and want you to have the same satisfaction they have felt in finding their dream. They are all about you! They instill a certain kind of confidence that you have within yourself what it takes to be a winner in your life by going for your dream.

You may be standing on a border right now. Looking back, you may see where your life has been. Up until this moment, it's been rather easy because you have been in your comfort zone. No challenges! No borders to cross! All familiar terrain. But deep down inside, there is something churning about your life, what you should do, who you should be. You have been on this threshold before, and stayed put. But staying put has not fulfilled your life. You have not claimed the dream. Not only do you not feel fulfilled, you fill like a coward, because you did not find the inner strength to cross the border to find your dream. You feel weak and spineless, disparaging towards yourself, even gutless.

But there is another person inside you who is just waiting to bust the border to a more fulfilling life. Indeed, that inner person is much stronger than you imagine. S/he is just waiting for you to give the word to go for your dream. Once you listen to this person and allow this person to pilot your life, you will find strength and courage, far more than you may have ever thought possible. And the thing of it is, that sense of empowerment and energy will just keep coming and coming. You will be proud of who you are and what your life has become. You will wonder why you ever stayed in the comfort zone or why you had any resistance to crossing the border to your dream. You will feel in your heart of hearts that your new found life and your fulfilled dream were all you were created to be. But it doesn't stop there. That is only the beginning. Your life is only beginning.

What about the people you left behind in the comfort zone? Will they be okay? Will they still love and care about you? They will be okay, because after all they are still in their comfort zone. Nothing will have changed for them. What's more? They will still love you. But one thing more—now they will not only love you, they will admire you. They will be so very proud that "one of theirs" had what it took to cross the border to find her/his dream. In fact, they will have a kind of vicarious ownership of you and your dream.

Do Good Anyway

Some years ago I came across "The Ten Paradoxical Commandments for Leadership." Over the years I have tucked these commandments away for safe-keeping, but from time to time bring them out and re-read as they always are a source of strength and focus. Anyone who has ever devoted himself/herself to a good cause or sought to make things better for the people in his/her sphere of influence, understands the need to rise above the criticism of small minds and destructive people.

The progress of humankind was never accomplished by "naysayers." Most every great effort of whatever nature was thwarted by those who said it could not be done and threw their stones. The good in the world has often been accomplished in the face of horrific opposition, and indeed, history has recorded its martyrs who have paid the ultimate sacrifice. Sometimes even a kind word or compassionate gesture is met with resistance and suspicion.

The challenge is always to rise above negativity, disapproval, and cynicism. It is not easy to go against the current or to be shot down when one's motive is worthy or noble. The temptation is to throw in the towel and adopt an attitude of "What's the use?" But true leaders never allow negativity to get the upper hand. The good never wins by surrendering heart, soul, or purpose. That is why one must always push on for truth, push on for a good cause, and push on for what is right. In the eyes of the world such a one may or may not wear a laurel, but in one's heart of hearts s/he knows what integrity and truth are all about. May you anchor your life in these paradoxical commandments of leadership:

(1) People are illogical, unreasonable, and self-centered. Love them anyway.

(2) If you do good, people will accuse you of selfish ulterior motives. Do good anyway.

(3) If you are successful, you win false friends and true enemies. Succeed anyway.

(4) The good you do today will be forgotten tomorrow. Do good anyway.

(5) Honesty and frankness make you vulnerable. Be honest and frank anyway.

(6) The biggest men with the biggest ideas can be shot down by the smallest men with the smallest minds. Think big anyway.

(7) People favor the underdogs but follow only the top dogs. Fight for the underdogs anyway.

(8) What you spend years building may be destroyed overnight. Build anyway.

(9) People really need help, but may attack you if you do help them. Help them anyway.

(10) Give the world the best you have and you'll get kicked in the teeth. Give the world the best you have anyway.[1]

Things That Offend

Why be offensive when offense is really unnecessary? We live in a multi-cultural, multi-ethnic, multi-heritage society and offense to someone's culture or heritage is not difficult, that is if we are insensitive.

---

[1] Kent Keith, The Paradoxical Commandments of Leadership, 1968.

But why intentionally offend someone? What gain is there in being offensive? How does offending another's race, ethnicity, or heritage promote harmony in the human family?

There are many icons that can arouse anger and alienation simply by mentioning them and remembering what they represent. Think, for instance, of the Confederate flag.

Having grown up in the South, I thought little about the flag when I was a child. I knew it was the flag of the Confederate states during the Civil War and that was about the extent of it. But the flag has in so many ways become a symbol—of heritage, pride, and yes, racism. Unfortunately, more of the latter as it is often understood as an ethnic/racial statement, more than one of heritage.

One has to wonder about the purpose of flying the Confederate flag and what statement one is making in flying it. Or what purpose is served by flying it over a capital lawn or including it on any official insignia, public or private? The Civil War was over long ago and we are one nation and one people. Displaying the flag even for the purpose of heritage sends the wrong message to a whole race of people who see the flag as racial provocation.

At the same time, the flap over the Confederate flag hanging from a noose on a thirteen-foot gallows in the

Mary Brogan Museum of Art in Tallahassee with the caption, "The Proper Way to Hang the Confederate Flag" was also indicative of provocation in reverse and insensitivity. Obviously, the artist, John Sims, knew his display would provoke anger and alienation from those who feel an alliance to their Southern heritage. So why do it? Why intentionally offend someone else as such can only polarize people rather than bring unity and harmony?

Provocation in reverse is also apparent in the NFL players who take the knee during the singing of the National Anthem. While participants claim they are making a statement about police brutality against people of color, such a display flies in the face of patriotic Americans, especially those who honor the sacrifice of over one million brave men and women who laid down their lives for their country or those who wear the blue and put their lives on the line every single day. Taking the knee has done far more to alienate people than it has to bring people together. Why not find a less "in your face" method of making a point?

There is a biblical admonition on being insensitive and offensive in Paul's letter to the Corinthians in Chapter 8. It is about meat being offered to idols. Paul says those who are of the faith know it really does not matter if the meat to be eaten has been offered to idols or not, because idols are just that—idols with no real meaning, but the catch is offending those who may not have the same understanding. Eating the meat could be a stumbling block and very offensive, so Paul asks: "Why do it?" There has to be a message here for symbols in our culture that are hot button icons. Why do it? Why be offensive just to make a point? Small wonder that Paul summarized all the concerns of the Corinthians with that beautiful statement in Chapter 13: "The greatest of these is love." Certainly, our world of insensitivity could learn a thing or two from Paul.

God and Golf

Living in southwest Florida and being a pastor, one cannot overlook two important matters in people's lives—church attendance and golf. People here appear to attend worship like few other places and tee times are filled to capacity throughout the week and even on Sunday mornings, that is unless it is raining. In most communities, a rainy day means church attendance is down as people simply stay home. It is just the opposite here. Most pastors might even pray for a rainy Sunday as the correlation between the weather and worship attendance is in reverse, meaning parishioners will come to church rather than hit the links.

Speaking of faith and golf, one cannot overlook their similarities with all the rules, obstacles, struggles, losses and victories. Such parallels are hard to miss.

At the outset, golf can keep you humble. The first of the Beatitudes addresses the concern of humility or being "poor in spirit." The importance of such a mindset is obvious and one does not have to wonder why it is first among the Beatitudes. No matter one's level of skill as a golfer, the first great lesson the game teaches is "not to think of one's self more highly than he ought to think." The game will always bring you to your knees. One should never think s/he has mastered the game, because just when you think you've conquered it, the next day out, you may play like you've never picked up a club.

The majority of golfers never take a lesson. Most golfers believe that just by picking up a club and practicing, they can conquer the game. It may come as a surprise, but only eight percent of those who play golf have ever had a lesson. Just a few lessons with a golfing pro can help a person with the fundamentals of such important concerns as stance, grip, swing, and keeping the eye on the ball. Neither can we manage the game of life without some coaching by the Master Teacher. He can help us understand that first and most important in the game of life is our stance. Our stance—what we believe and what we stand for—affects everything in life, the decisions we make and how we will live our days.

A second fundamental is our grip. An improper grip will do anything but keep the ball on course. By gripping the club incorrectly, one loses control. In life, we must also have the proper grip, or life also spins out of control. Pros may say we are gripping the club too tightly or too loosely. In life we must also have to be mindful of what we may be holding too tightly or too loosely. Such is critical to reaching our goal.

The pro will tell us to keep our eye on the ball. The most fundamental error is taking your eye off the ball, creating an errant shot. People of faith must also keep their focus on the One who can keep our lives on course. We are to "look to Jesus, the author and finisher of our faith." Hebrews 12:2. Keeping our eyes on him will keep our lives on course.

Finally, there is the matter of honesty. Unlike other sports where there are referees and umpires, honesty in golf is up to each individual. There are a thousand and one ways to fudge on the score and no one will know, that is no one but you. It's up to each player to play by the rules and keep an honest score. John Freeman said, "You can tell a lot about a person, even a total stranger, by playing a round of golf with him."

A person of integrity will be honest on both fairways—those of golf or those of life.

The Ten Commandments of Marriage

I.   Thou shalt understand what marriage really is.

What is marriage? In some circles of the church, it is one of the Seven Sacraments. In other communions it is thought of as a covenant or rite of the church. It is a legal binder as marriage is recorded with the Clerk of

Court. It is all of these, but one thing more—when you find the right person, it is the Gift of God.

II. Thou shalt accept each other as the other is.

We never marry someone expecting to tweak or change their personality after we are married. As we have come to know and love them, it was for their unique personality and content of character that attracted us to them. That makes the one we love unique and so very special. We always accept and love the one we married just the way s/he is.

III. Thou shalt talk things through.

We live in this amazing world of communication. Who would have believed all the ways we can send a message instantly with the internet, cell phones, text messages—it is all beyond belief, this world of communication, but nowhere on earth is communication more important than between a husband and wife. While disagreements may be few and far between, before we go to sleep at night we must resolve the issues by talking things through.

IV. Thou shalt trust one another.

If marriage is about anything, it is about trust. No one wants to live in an atmosphere of suspicion, but rather an atmosphere of loving trust. We must trust one another completely and without reservation. Even if trust were ever misplaced, we are a thousand times better off in an atmosphere of trust than one of suspicion.

V. Thou shalt forgive one another.

We marry "for better or for worse," meaning we understand upfront there are no perfect people. Even the people we love will make mistakes, but that is what marriage is about, forgiving, embracing, and moving forward.

VI. Thou shalt keep a sense of humor.

It has often been found that humor creates a bond like nothing else. Humor is joy and joy is love. We must allow there to be a great deal of humor in this marriage. Let there be laughter every day. Laugh much and laugh often. It will create a bond.

VII. Thou shalt be loyal to one another.

"For this cause a man shall leave his father and his mother and be joined to his wife," so say the scriptures. But let a wife also leave. Let no one stand between this bond. Let a man know that even if he is wrong, his wife is in his corner, and let a wife know that her husband is always by her side.

VIII. Thou shalt cultivate a romance.

As we come to know each other, we do all the little extras to win love and affection—the way we look, cards, flowers, evenings out, phone calls, and words—it's all about cultivating a romance. But the wedding is the beginning of romance. How will it be in the future, ten, twenty, or fifty years down the way. It just gets better and better as the years go by as we cultivate a romance.

IX.   Thou shalt take the positive approach.

Nothing creates a mindset like a positive approach. It is true in life and especially true in marriage. When we wake up in the morning and say it is going to be a beautiful day, it always is. If we say "This is going to be the best marriage ever, it will be just that—the best marriage ever.

X.   Thou shalt make thine a Christian marriage.

While we know there is no "magic" about our faith in God and including God in our life's journey, we know that those who welcome God to be a part of their journey, God will bless in a very special way. Make yours a Christian marriage and God will bless your lives.

CHAPTER 2

The Colors of Growth and Development in Your Community of Faith

Marketing Your Church

The folks on Madison Avenue do not have the inside track on marketing, but we can learn a great deal from them, and in fact, grow our churches by applying those same techniques, approaches that make us want whatever product they are peddling. Marketing is not a new term for the church, although we are reluctant to think of growing the church in terms of "marketing." But we all market our church at some level, whether just speaking well of it, or having an intentional plan to grow church membership through a diversified approach, including the use of media in whatever form.

Every church can grow its membership, whether rural or urban, large or small, traditional or contemporary. It is only a matter of applying certain principles which are time-proven.

Question: Why do you buy a certain product and possibly pay more for it than another product of equal value, and perhaps at less cost? Why do the New York Yankees have such a following of fans? Why is there a waiting list to obtain a seat in Lambeau Field to watch the Green Bay Packers? It is all the same basic reason. Marketing plants a thought in our heads that one product is superior to another, and people like to follow winning teams. Both the teams we root for and the products we buy are reflections of who we see ourselves to be. It's a lot about our self-image in purchasing a product or rooting for a team that makes us feel good about ourselves.

While we may not want to admit it, the same principle is true of why people are attracted to one church over another. Our church is an extension of who we see ourselves to be, and while we want to believe there are more virtuous reasons for choosing a particular church, our self-image and what we have been led to believe about a particular church, do come into play, far more than we might wish to admit.

So why market your church? First of all, you are marketing the church to its own membership. Whatever form of marketing a church chooses to promote its programs, it will discover the very first people to receive the message are the people themselves. Marketing is a stimulus that energizes people and gets them excited about themselves and their own church. When the energy starts flowing, good things begin to happen. Members get on board and begin to promote their church. When the energy flow starts streaming, people feel it. Just like the products we buy or the winning teams we like to identify with, church folk will get excited about their church. Truth is: If the members of a church are not excited, who will be?

Secondly, marketing draws attention! Period! Exclamation point! We never think about the media that is flowing into our living rooms or dens, or that is on the air waves every day. We are not even conscious we are being influenced by the marketing gurus, but the subliminal message is being planted. When we go to a store, consider buying a car, or pull for a team, we are already programmed to go in a certain direction, and we don't even know it. The same principle works in growing a church. People do not come to you. You must go to them. You must develop a plan and stick to it. It's a guarantee: a pro-active church that "markets its wares" will always grow.

There are many approaches to marketing: social media, radio spots, billboards, newspaper ads, televising the services, impact cards, newsletters, electronic newsletters, attendance campaigns, free "stuff," visitations, press releases (free), Constant Contact, email blasts, free food, a "Thought for the Day." The important thing is to get the church's name and program opportunities in front of people. Marketing gets people excited and it grows the church.

The very best and most cost effective form of church marketing is that of social media. Utilizing a social media expert in your church will yield untold results, especially with younger people. The biggest form of social media are social networks that include Facebook, Twitter, LinkedIn. Media sharing sites consist of Instagram, YouTube, and Snapchat. How do these social media sites work and what are the functions of each?

SOCIAL NETWORKS include Facebook, Twitter, and LinkedIn. These are used to connect with people and are sometimes called "relationship networks." They enable people to share information and ideas. With the introduction of the mobile internet, these networks have become hubs that transform nearly every aspect of modern life in whatever social experience someone would like to share. In terms of church life, such simple events as a pot luck dinner can be shared to hundreds of people. This network can also promote services, concerts, or special events, both before the event and as a celebration after the event. As people "like" what you have posted on Facebook, that information can travel to a host of friends, people you do not even know.

MEDIA SHARING NETWORKS share photos, videos, live video, and other media online. Live casting or live streaming is often the term used that describes the process of broadcasting real-time, live video footage or video feed to an audience accessing the video stream over the internet. The viewing device can be a desktop computer, laptop, tablet, smart phone or digital screen. The broadcast can be just video, audio or both. What a great way to share a worship service with a wider audience, or members who may be homebound or are away from the community!

A BLOG (shortening of "weblog") is an online journal or informational website displaying information in the reverse chronological order, with latest posts appearing first. It is a platform where a writer or even a group of writers share their views on an individual subject. The differential factor of a blog is that of feedback from visitors. Conversational posts encourage interaction with blog guests. At the end of every blog article, readers can share their different opinions.

While social media appeals to those familiar with the tools of the internet, more traditional ways of marketing are still of great value. such a simple thing as mailing out unused bulletins to members who may not have shown up on Sunday is worth far more than the effort. Newsletters should always be exciting, positive, and upbeat—a lot less copy and a lot more pictures of people involved in ministry. People love to get newsletters from their church, but more than just "getting a newsletter," they love to hear the exciting things that are happening. After all, since it is "their" church, it is "them," who they are. The homebound especially read newsletters "word for word." Constant Contact and email blasts are inexpensive ways to get messages out. Grow those lists! Just go to ConstantContact.com and you will be on the way to staying in touch on a weekly basis at a nominal cost.

IMPACT CARDS are a way of reaching thousands of people with a personal message about your church on a colorful 5 1/2 X 8 1/2 post card. There are companies that create and mail these to any zip code you choose.

Finally, remember: "Beginning is half the job." By the time you take it through every committee and board of the church, it might take six months or longer and people lose their enthusiasm. Also remember: "Every person is a prospect." Just do it! Make it happen and you'll be glad you did!

To Grow or Not to Grow

A slight variation of Shakespeare's famous quote, *"To be or not to be, that is the question,"* takes on meaning when scripted in terms of church growth, *"To grow or not to grow, that is the question."* The only problem is that it's not the question as "not to grow" with reference to the life of a church has grave consequences. Given, all churches cannot grow and some struggle with declining congregations as agrarian communities or small towns that were once the centerpieces of life and religion have either disappeared or are vanishing from the profile of church life in America. However, not to grow or even to "maintain" can be a death sentence to a once thriving congregation. In most cases there are measures which can be taken to halt the membership and attendance decline.

So often in older congregations the individuals who were once the driving forces for life and energy are tired, "whipped," or just simply feel they have done their part and now it's someone else's turn. While that may be true, there must be a strategy to turn over leadership and find new life or the church they have worked so hard to uphold over the years will continue its decline until the day comes when the doors are shut and the church is no more. But let's not be fatalistic. Any church can grow if there is a population resource, that is if there are people in a given area who may attend. It is only a matter of applying tried and proven principles of church growth. Here are nine ways to enhance the growth of any church:

1. Develop a Positive Self-image of the Church.

Churches are like people: they have personalities and a sense of self-worth. Just as people are drawn to individuals with positive self-images, they are also drawn to churches which radiate positive feelings about themselves. Who wants to attend a church where all they hear is how bad things are or that "people aren't coming like they used to." Talking down the church, the pastor, the music, or the church in general, will only weaken the church further and ultimately push people away. Talking up the church makes people feel good not only about their place of worship, but themselves as churches are extensions of the people themselves.

2. Create an Atmosphere of Energy.

Go into some churches and you immediately feel energized. Go in other churches and you wonder when they are going to call in the undertaker. Why the difference? It's all about energy. Some churches create energy and others seem to kill it. Positive energy attracts people while a lack of energy sends the message that things are dismal. This is why the stadiums of winning teams are always full and tickets are always available for those that have a poor record. We live in an energized world and people want to feel energy when they come to their place of worship. Energy is created by upbeat messages and services so that when folks leave the church they feel inspired and ready to face the world, rather than simply having gone through a process of lifeless rote liturgies, prayers, and messages. Energy is contagious, and it does bring people!

3. Market Your Wares.

Advertising always pays. The advertising pitch in whatever form creates a feeling of anticipation. It's like a kid waiting for Christmas morning. The anticipation of it outweighs the event itself. Church advertising, like that created on Madison Avenue, has to tickle the sense of wonder so that the recipient just has to have the product or the experience. Anticipation creates a sense of expectation from the prospective attendee even before they approach the door of the church. You are indeed "one step ahead" in generating an atmosphere of exciting worship. There are multiple ways to market the church, but the secret of it all is that of creating a profile of the church so that when a prospect thinks of attending worship s/he will be drawn to yours, without ever knowing why. The internet has put marketing the church at the fingertips of any church. It is only a matter of developing an active website, sending email blasts, or creatively thinking of ways to get the word out. Newspaper ads and radio spots are ways to keep the name and activities of a local church before the public. Most newspapers welcome press releases about events in local churches and this is a service that is free. Impact cards to targeted zip codes are relatively inexpensive ways to send your message to thousands of households. The secret of advertising is to do it repetitively as studies show that a one-time shot has little effect, but multiple messages plant the seeds of interest.

4. Identify and Follow-up Visitors.

The fact that someone has visited your church is an expression s/he already has an interest. Something has ignited their interest; otherwise they would not be there. Or it could be like a clerk in a department store asking if you need help. Unless you really have something in mind, you may respond "Just looking." This happens in church shopping as well. Sometimes visitors are "just looking," but they are shopping your church among others. The "cardinal sin" of growing a church is to have a visitor come and leave and s/he is not given a warm welcome or identified for follow-up. People tend to gravitate towards people they know. Established churches find numerous circles of friends who have things in common. Although not intended, such circles are "closed communities," and visitors feel either excluded or unwelcome. This can be overcome through greeters or a welcome committee whose responsibility it is to identify visitors, introduce them to friends, obtain their contact information, and be sure their visit is followed-up with a phone call, letter, or visit.

5. Stay in Touch with the Membership.

Staying in touch with members is of utmost importance as they can become inactive or even have an illness that needs the caring response of the church. A member that is absent for several Sundays is a red flag that something is wrong and s/he needs a call. Members, particularly the homebound, love to receive a newsletter from their church. Newsletters, like the services themselves, should be upbeat and lively. More pictures than copy creates a sense of life and things happening. Sending the Sunday's left-over bulletins doubles not only as information, but a reminder to the member that s/he was missed. The easiest and most inexpensive way to stay in touch is Constant Contact, an internet program that provides ready-made templates for every occasion. Constant Contact can personalize each email as if written personally to the recipient, no matter how many are on the contact list.

6. Create an Atmosphere of Joy.

Church services must project a sense of joy and excitement. While people don't come to church to be entertained, life in the 21st Century is fast-moving and stimulating and worship must be the same. Worship that is not creative and moving can become dull, and boring, and minutes into the service people are wondering, "how much longer is this going to last?" Joyful and exciting worship keeps people involved and inspired. Remember: *"Make a joyful noise unto the Lord, all ye lands."*

7. Be a Care-giving Congregation.

People need care and part of the mission of the church is to give them care. Love them. Support them. Reach out to them. Be concerned about their pain, illnesses, grief, sorrow, loneliness. Churches should never leave all the care-giving to the pastor. The most effective way to offer care is through an organized plan whether through the deacons or some committee whose responsibility it is to embrace those in need with the care and concern of the church.

8. Be Open to Special Services.

Special services like weddings, baptisms, and funerals, are opportunities for the church to extend the ministry of Christ in a time of need. Churches that adopt policies that someone must be a member of the church in order to have the services of the church miss huge opportunities for ministry. The church is unique in its capacity to serve these special needs. People will remember if they are "turned away," or "welcomed," in a celebratory or time of need in their lives.

9. Be Open to Opportunities for Mission.

People are innately good and want to do good with the resources they have. When given the opportunity, they will be generous in terms of giving to a worthy cause. It is important to identify the cause and how their gift will be of value in answering the need. If possible, it is good to in some way connect people to the cause. It is also imperative that they be recognized or thanked for the good they have done.

These principles of church growth work when applied. What can be more exciting for any church member than to see his/her church come to life with energy, joy, and new people. Try these principles and it's a promise your church will find new life and grow its membership.

The Changing Landscape of Church Life

If you are old enough, you may remember the days of church life in the 1950's and '60's. Going to church and heeding its message was the norm. Unfortunately, those days are gone as the message of the church no longer holds a prominent place of authority and influence in America. Researchers are categorizing and quantifying people groups who dismiss the church and the faith it preaches. The Pew Research Center recently found that roughly 20% of the American population does not affiliate with any religious organization.

Categorically these people are called "nones," and it appears the church is losing ground to this trend. The "nones" are the un-churched who reject the church's claim to moral and religious authority. Unsettling for those of the faith is that approximately 36% of these "nones" are Millennials, born between 1985–2000.

There is another group that has dropped out of church life known as the "dones." While the "dones" are people of faith, they are rejecting organized religion due to issues of bureaucracy, judgment, church fights, and the pain the church often places on its members. While they manage their personal faith, they do it outside the institutional church. They are "done" with organized religion.

If local congregations are to be effective, they must faithfully respond to this changing cultural environment. How can this happen?

Tried and proven methods of church life that worked in the past may not work anymore, so the church must adapt to new ways of reaching people in this changing culture. Leonard Wong, an instructor for the U.S. Army, says that today's army must adapt to the changing environments in the theater of war. A key phase from Dr. Wong is that "leaders spend less time fretting...and more time exploiting opportunities."

So the question in your local church is what opportunities present themselves to reach out to those who no longer find the church relevant? To move forward, we must "think outside the box." Discover those opportunities and allow the church to reach beyond itself.

Pastor Assassinators Are All Too Familiar

Terrorism has become a much too familiar term in the modern world. It is a method of warfare whereby a relatively small group of terrorists through acts of violence seek to intimidate and terrorize a much larger group of people for political ends. It is quite different from traditional types of warfare where the enemy was clearly defined. Terrorism is executed by sick and evil people whose purpose it is to destroy at all costs.

Unfortunately, terrorism exists in the church, just in a different form, although the principles of intimidation are all present. The target is some unsuspecting pastor who is faithfully doing his/her work of ministry and seeking to build the church. It's a kind of game with the folks who carry it out, but a very dangerous one, one that not only brings horrific pain to the pastor, but to the entire church. Lloyd Rediger (*Clergy Journal*, August, 1993) appropriately referred to these terror-ists as "Clergy Killers." They exist in most every church, although they are masters at keeping them-selves and their dirty work concealed. Seldom do they ever surface, but the effects of their work in the lives of pastors and churches are catastrophic.

Pastors mysteriously resign, move on, or leave the ministry, and no one ever seems to know why or take the time to investigate. Many parishioners nonchalant-ly roll over and accept the plight of what happened to their pastor as a matter of course. "S/he must have done something wrong," or "It doesn't affect me, so why get involved." While they may empathize with the pastor, challenging the terrorists is too risky. Roll-overs are, however, just as guilty as those who do the dirty work against the unsuspecting pastor because their silence is nothing more than consent. But as long as these religious thugs go unchallenged, they will keep on doing their evil deeds against pastors.

These predators who feed on pastors camouflage themselves and their motives extremely well. They come on as "religious," and always acting "for the good of the church." They never fight fair and will stoop to any level of subversion to get their way and destroy the pastor, all under the guise of "good church members." They are often people who feel threatened by the high regard of the pastor among parishioners and community and conclude "S/he is getting too powerful."

Pastors are vulnerable. They are called to be pastors and called to serve. They are not schooled in the tactics of these malicious saboteurs who take aim and destroy lives. Since the saboteurs know pastors will not stoop to their own unethical levels and will always operate above board and with honesty and integrity, they know pastors are easy prey and once out of the picture, they will again be back in control.

The *modus operandi* of pastor assassinators includes such methods as: (1) Making the pastor feel s/he has done something wrong, (2) Wearing down the pastor's resistance, (3) Planting seeds of discontent about the pastor within the congregation, (4) Seizing positions of power within church, (5) Sabotaging the pastor's leadership, (6) Harassment, and, (7) Questioning the pastor's mental state.

Pastor assassinators are usually motivated by their own sense of omnipotence. They see themselves as "the leaders," "the ones who know best," and "the ones who must take things into their own hands." They broker their power with their checkbook—"we could never lose their support," manipulation of others, intimidation, and, yes, grace and hospitality. They are such artisans at "schmoozing," few realize they are being courted with ulterior motives.

Pastor assassinations will go on into an indefinite future as long as the terrorists go unchecked and unchallenged. They back off for a while and wait for the next victim, even if they have had a part in bringing that pastor to the pulpit. The best strategy to thwart pastor assassinations is to: (1) Stand up for the pastor and come to his/her defense, (2) Ensure that strong advocates for the pastor are on pastor/parish committee, (3) Expose the pastor assassinators for what and who they are, (4) Challenge the rollovers to be guided by Christian conviction and not by opportunity or convenience. (5) Follow the church's by-laws when a pastor's leadership is brought into question, never allowing a small group of disgruntled members to secretly bring down a pastor who has the support of the larger congregation.

Double Standard for Clergy

In terms of moral standards, should more be expected from clergypersons than the general population within faith communities? The question of double standards is nothing new, even though recent settlements of clergy abuse cases have brought the issue into the limelight. The fact that young Timothy was admonished to "be an example to believers in speech and conduct" (I Timothy 4:12) would lead one to conclude that even in the infancy of the church, the question of exemplar behavior by those set aside for spiritual leadership was a concern of great importance.

A landmark study by Baylor University published in *The Journal of Scientific Study of Religion*, (December, 2009), conducted among 3,500 adults, concluded that sexual misconduct among clergy is more prevalent than most people believe. The across the board study of pastors, priests, and rabbis, found that 3.1% of cases observed by those who attend religious services at least once a month, have been victims of clergy sexual misconduct. The overall aim of the study was to prompt congregations to consider policies that would protect their members from leaders who abuse their power.

These spiritual leaders are in unique roles in terms of trust, charisma, and power. They are often viewed as "God's representatives," whose authority and actions are above reproach. Concomitant with the position is a sense of trustworthiness and moral admiration that may be embellished by personal charisma and charm. But violating boundaries of morality in whatever form by clergypersons is destructive to the victims, the violators, and the religious community in general. Such should always be addressed by those in authority.

People do have a right to look to their pastor, priest, or rabbi for moral leadership. Part of the vow of ordination is to live an exemplary life. If one is going to "talk the talk" s/he must also "walk the walk." At the same time, there can be no rejoicing when a spiritual leader falls.

When one who is set aside through ordination is found guilty of misconduct, the religious judicatory with oversight must take the offense seriously, address the offender appropriately, and reach out to the victim. Such offenses cannot be denied or swept under the rug. Further, should the same grace offered any child of God who has fallen, not also be extended to those spiritual leaders who have fallen with the hope that the message of grace may in time be the message of redemption.

Healthy Churches Manage Pastoral Relations

Nothing is more destructive in the life of a congregation than conflict over the pastor's leadership and tenure and how that concern is addressed and processed. Nothing will divide a church more quickly. Nothing will galvanize feelings of enmity between former friends as abruptly and permanently. Nothing will polarize a congregation with such certainty. It is therefore of utmost importance that guidelines be set in place and followed in dealing with such an emotionally-charged concern as pastoral relations and tenure. Churches that fail to do this are in for rough seas, division, horrendous pain, and alienation they never dreamed possible.

Discontent over the pastor's leadership usually begins with a very small group who see themselves as "leaders," "the ones who know best," "the ones who must take action."

While they conceal their motives, most often their ultimate goal is to dismiss the pastor. They see the pastor as expendable and begin to set a plan in place to accomplish their goal. They secretly form coalitions and seek to enlarge the circle of dissatisfaction. They plant seeds of malcontent. They always claim they are acting "for the good of the church." A cancer is formed. A malignancy begins to spread. A once healthy happy church begins a struggle for life.

The pain and destruction of mismanaging pastoral relations and power brokering approaches go very deep and across the board. While the epicenter is the pastor and the pastor's family, the ripple effects reach far beyond and affect the lives of entire memberships. One young lady, reflecting on such a mismanaged experience, said nothing in her life hurt her more deeply than what her church did to the pastor she loved. Others may react by simply distancing themselves from the church, feeling such approaches are inappropriate for any community, but especially the community of faith. Others just walk away and never return to the church or any church.

There are ways of addressing concerns over pastoral leadership that preserve the health of the pastor and the congregation. Having well defined guidelines in place and following those guidelines is the best way to avoid hurt and alienation. Preventive medicine is always better than treatment once an illness has set in. Here are some time-proven strategies to preserve a healthy church in terms of pastoral relations:

1. Make sure the by-laws of the church clearly define the call and terms of tenure of the pastor, and follow those by-laws. Any church that does not include such policy in their rules of governance exposes itself to internal strife when the pastor's leadership is called into question. By-laws are safeguards put in place long before times of need.

2. Follow the by-laws. Stepping outside the established guidelines is asking for trouble. Allowing control groups to usurp power and make decisions regarding the tenure of the pastor will mushroom into an all-out "church war," which will bring division and untold consequences that may never be healed. A handful of people who take things into their own hands can destroy a church.

3. Establish a strong Pastoral Relations Committee that is a conduit for grievances and resolving differences. Such a committee should be comprised of strong and mature personalities who are able to make unbiased judgments through mediation and resolution. Such a committee is able to "contain" concerns in a confidential setting which preserves integrity as well as preventing metastasizing strife into the larger church.

4. Bring in trained and knowledgeable consultants who offer skills to resolve issues for which the church may be poorly equipped to handle. Such intervention can address concerns and defuse issues in their infancy. Paying trained consultants is a small price to pay compared to the horrific and often irreparable damage done to a congregation or a pastor.

Every church has issues and often those concerns fester around the pastor. Resolving those matters in a mature and honest way will preserve the health of the church and ensure its continued strength and ministry. If you want a better pastor, pray for the one you have.

Who Governs the Church?

Who governs your church? A bishop? A presbytery? A church council? The congregation at large? This sounds like an innocuous question and someone may respond that it really does not matter. S/he may say, "I

go to church to worship and express my persoₙₗ
in a fellowship of believers." While the latter is true,
historically few things have raised the ire of the faithful more than the question of church polity. In fact,
there has been far more division over church government than over theology. Whatever place of worship
you belong to, you can be sure there is some form of
governance well set in place, and that that issue was
settled long before the church began to think about
matters of faith. Church government does matter,
even to those who think it does not.

There are three basic types of church government: the
episcopacy, the presbytery, and the congregational
and each, to some measure, traces its governing practices to the New Testament church. For example,
those who see an episcopacy type of government look
to the function of the apostles who passed authority to
govern on to bishops. In the very earliest times, the
Council of Jerusalem elected presbyters as leaders and
decision makers for the church.

The episcopacy, the most universal form of church
government, is a method of government in which authority lies with the bishop who oversees a given judicatory or area of governance. Both the Roman
Catholic Church and the Anglican Church (Episcopal)
practice a form of government in which the bishop is
the seat of authority for a given diocese. The Methodists, who popularized the faith through revivalism, also
kept the episcopacy as a form of church government;

hence the very name, Methodist, implies a method of government with a presiding bishop and centralized form of government.

Presbyterian churches are independent of each other, but have in common the acceptance of the Westminster Confession and practice a Presbyterian form of government. The local congregation elects its "session" which governs the local church's affairs. The session is led by the minister, "the teaching elder" who is called by the congregation. The minister is, however, ordained by the presbytery which consists of the teaching and ruling elders from a group of congregations. Hence, governing authority is shared by the local and larger church.

Congregationalism is a system of church government that appeared after the Reformation by parties that rejected the idea of a state church and saw believers as a "gathered" church, independent of bishops and magistrates, and not subject to outside authority. Each local church had the right to ordain its ministers, govern its own affairs, and own its own property. Congregationalism as a form of church government is much wider than the church that bears its name. Baptists, among others who function on a more independent basis, usually follow a congregational form of government.

Most every church will be governed by one of these three methods of government or a modification of such. Understanding how your church is governed will enable you to participate at a more informed level.

Protocol in Addressing Your Pastor

Church members are often puzzled, if not sometimes a bit uneasy, about how to address their pastor; i.e., Reverend, Pastor, Father, Mr., Ms, Dr., or Rabbi in the case of the Jewish faith. Protocol changes from denomination to denomination. For instance, Lutherans always address their clergyperson as "Pastor," while other communions prefer the title, "Reverend." Growing up, my parents always called the pastor "Mr." or "Rev," and we were forbidden to address the pastor otherwise. But things are changing. We feel more familiar with our clergyperson and often dismiss titles for a preferred first name basis.

The uncertainty of protocol is not an issue in some faith communities. Roman Catholics refer to the ordained as "Father" when addressing the pastor. Episcopalians may also use the term "Father," but most often refer to minister as "Reverend." United Methodists and Baptists address their pastor as both "Reverend" and as "Pastor." Presbyterians almost always use the term, "Reverend." With the world becoming less formal, parishioners may feel they wish to address their pastor in a less formal way, simply using his/her given name so the pastor is addressed as "Pastor Jim," or "Reverend Jane."

Some pastors have advanced and honorary degrees. An earned degree may be a PhD or Doctor of Ministry and an honorary degree is a Doctor of Divinity conferred by a university for outstanding work in ministry. The title "Reverend" refers to ordination and the title "Doctor" refers to degrees.

My rule of thumb is that titles should never separate or distance pastors from their people. Sometimes we do need our pastor to be a "Reverend," or a "Pastor," and at other times simply a friend. Why not allow the moment or need to define the protocol?

Applause in Church

"To applaud or not to applaud?" that is the question. What is appropriate in worship? That question seems to be a sleeper and both pastors and lay people sometimes question whether applause is appropriate in worship. The question surfaced in my church some months ago, as it did in the last four churches I served as pastor. While people want to express their joy and appreciation for the inspiration given, they also want to maintain some sense of reverence during the service and wonder whether they should express their gratitude through what seems natural: applause.

The question of applause surfaces in both Catholic and protestant communions and there is diversity within those communions which usually comes down to perceptions and practices within local congregations. A few years ago, the issue reached such a level, the Session of First Presbyterian Church of Roanoke, VA, requested their Worship Committee research and present a position paper on applause in church. You may Google the church's conclusions, which are grounded both in scripture and cultural practice.

Some months ago I sent a survey to a number of my ministerial colleagues in Naples which included mainline Protestant, Roman Catholic, and independent churches. The results were somewhat as I expected, that the issue of applause had surfaced in their particular parishes and there was some feeling about whether or not congregants should applaud. Some of the responses are as follows:

> The issue of applause had surfaced in most churches surveyed.
>
> Attitudes vary about applause within the congregation.

There are times when applause seems always the appropriate response such as when children or youth sing, or there is some moment of joy that cannot be expressed in any other way.

Applause should always be offered as gratitude to God and not as an expression to musicians or those leading worship.

One pastor friend did relate that the issue of applause in church was a question settled many years ago and that those who objected simply found another place to worship. All parts of the service, including baptisms, were applauded.

There are biblical references to applause such as those found in Psalm 47 "Clap your hands, all people," or Isaiah 55:12 "All the trees of the field shall clap their hands." Since most churches do not openly shout "Amen," or "Hallelujah" any more, perhaps applause is simply another way of expressing approval and joy. There is no "right" or "wrong" about applause in worship, only what seems an appropriate expression of joy as led by the Spirit.

Sunday Morning Competition

Most of us remember a time when Sunday mornings were reserved for worship or a family outing, if the latter be the case. How times have changed of recent with the constant pressure being placed on kids to participate in activities which bring them in conflict with worship or family, namely sports, recreation, or activities for which there is no other time slot available! My question to those who plan sports and other activities on Sunday mornings and demand the time of youth, is what message is being sent to kids and families regarding the development of their faith and spiritual journey. Simply put: What happened to the sanctity of Sunday morning?

Demand for kids' time and the pressure placed on them to participate during a time that has traditionally been reserved for worship and family can be outrageous. Look at it from a kid's perspective. The coach or activity leader says you have a game or practice on Sunday morning. Failure to show up will have consequences, like "not being on the team," or "riding the pine," or some dramatic consequence from the youth's perspective. Given a choice between pleasing the coach and the options of worship or family time, what choice does the kid have?

Sports teams and activities directors have six days a week to have youth at their disposal, and even six and a half if one counted Sunday afternoons. Why must things be planned on Sunday mornings which demand the time of kids who would profit far more by spending some time either in worship or some quality time with their families? It is not at all fair to kids to place them is such an uncompromising position.

What can be done about this new phenomenon? Two things actually: (1) Sports and activities people can respect Sunday morning and plan their events at some other time. (2) Parents, who are the ultimate authority in managing family time can "put their foot down," in preserving Sunday morning either for worship or for family. There is, after all, a window of opportunity in every child's life to instill values and faith, and once that opportunity is passed, it will not come again. *"For physical training is of some value, but godliness has value for all things, holding promise for both the present life and the life to come."* I Timothy 4:8 NIV.

CHAPTER 3

The Colors of Patriotism and Polarization in America

The Land of the Free and the Home of the Brave

We hear those stirring words all the time: "The land of the free and the home of the brave." These heartfelt expressions are oft quoted in sermons, political speeches, and rallying points of patriotism. This phrase touches something deep down inside all those who love America, its freedom, and appreciate those brave souls who made the "first down payment" and others who have made the installments along the way to keep her free. It is a provocative phrase. But who first coined the phrase? It was none less than Francis

Scott Key, the author of what we now know as "The Star Spangled Banner."

An attorney, author, and amateur poet from Georgetown, thirty-five-year-old Key accompanied by John Skinner, a British prisoner exchange agent, boarded a British flagship outside the Baltimore Harbor hoping to negotiate the release of a friend. The 80-gun flagship was part of a large armada of 18 warships overlooking Fort McHenry in the Chesapeake Bay. This was only weeks after the British had attacked Washington, burning the Capital, the Treasury, and the President's home. Neither Skinner nor Key were allowed to return to their sloop as they now knew the strength and positions of the British fleet ready to clobber the American fort. All these two could do during the night of September 13, 1814, was to sit on board the British ship and watch the embattled fort receive no less than 1500 rounds of rockets and bombs for twenty-five heart-rending hours.

The sounds of the cannons were excruciating. The light from the bursting rockets over the fort was conclusive the fort would fall. "It seemed as though mother earth had opened and was vomiting shot and shell in a sheet of fire and brimstone," Key would later write. From such a barrage he was certain the Union Jack would be flying over the fort come dawn. From his vantage point, when the sun's rays first fell across the fort, to Key's surprise and joy, the banner of stars and stripes, not the Union Jack, was still waving. As the son of a patriot in the Continental Army, the sight must have made his chest swell with pride.

Light from the unremitting bombardment of rockets and bombs gave Key a visual of the banner of broad stripes and bright stars that seemed embedded in his heart and soul. After his release, he made his way back to Baltimore where he quickly put the impression to pen with a poem he entitled, "The Defence of Fort M'Henry." The poem was published on September 21, 1814, only days after Key had completed it, and was soon put to a popular tune, "To Anacreon in Heaven," by John Stafford Smith.

Key was a devoutly religious man and almost became an Episcopal priest, rather than an attorney. His writings were usually sprinkled with biblical references. He was instrumental in founding several parishes around Baltimore and Washington. He also helped found two Episcopal seminaries. Although it is only the first verse of his poem that is sung as, "The Star Spangled Banner," the poem actually has three verses and his religious leanings are particularly noted in the third stanza. Each stanza ends with those enduring words, "the land of the free and the home of the brave."

Anyone who loves this country is touched when that phrase is spoken or sung. Like Francis Scott Key, the words bring a visual, whether seeing the flag draped over the coffin of a fallen soldier, folded and given to a surviving widow with words of "a grateful nation," placed beside grave markers at Arlington, flying over the nation's capital, spread the entire breadth and length of a football field, planted on the moon's surface on each of the Apollo's landings (1969-1972), or the most vivid image of the six marines hoisting the stars and stripes atop Mount Suribachi on Iwo Jima. It's an image! It's a visual! It represents so much!

Just think of it: America is the land of the free. Nowhere on earth is freedom more apparent or manifest than in this land whose boundaries are from sea to shining sea, but whose opportunities know no boundary at all. In America, one is free to live his/her life in whatever manner one chooses, express faith in a chosen place of worship or not worship if that is the choice, gather in an open assembly, decide truth from a free press unencumbered by a dictatorial government, or petition the government if that is a need.

America is also the home of the brave. The strong stance taken by those defending Fort McHenry has been replicated time and again in our nation's history, whether at Gettysburg, Meuse-Argonne (WWI), Normandy (WWII), Heartbreak Ridge (Korea), Khe Sanh (Vietnam), Fallujah (Iraq), Kabul (Afghanistan), or the hundreds of other places untold bravery has been exhibited by those defending America's freedom.

Perhaps with bias, it must be said the American flag is the most beautiful and meaningful flag among the nations on earth. Its stripes represent the thirteen original colonies and its stars the now fifty states that comprise its union. It is a "grand old flag, a high flying flag, the emblem of the land I love, the home of the free and the brave." Yes, Francis Scott Key got it right: It is "the land of the free and the home of the brave."

Who Were the Pilgrims

Pilgrims and Thanksgiving go together, but who were "the Pilgrims?" They were more than legends. They were, in fact, real people who were at odds with the Church of England which had broken away from the Roman Catholic Church in 1534 when King Henry VIII declared himself to be the head of the church. They were referred to as "Separatists," as all they wanted was a separate church that adhered to simpler practices of worship, without the prescribed structured forms of worship.

To literally separate from the Church of England was a radical movement as such a fracture would fly in the face of the king and his ecclesiastical hierarchy. Because of their resistance, some were fined and even imprisoned. When the group could no longer endure the harassment, they left their homes and moved to Leiden in the Dutch Netherlands where they remained for twelve years. Although they were under the leadership of Pastor John Robinson who taught theology at the University of Leiden, life was immensely brutal as they were unwelcome immigrants.

It was at the suggestion of Pastor Robinson that the group began to set their eyes on the New World, thinking in particular of coming to the already established Virginia colony as it extended all the way to the Hudson Valley. To finance the voyage, they formed a joint stock company of investors who would be repaid with interest from the trading profits of the colony.

Two ships, the *Mayflower* and the *Speedwell*, left England on August 15, 1620. However, the *Speedwell* was taking on water, so both ships had to return and a number of passengers on the *Speedwell* boarded the *Mayflower* and set sail on September 6, 1620. The group of 102 passengers and 26 crewmen arrived on Cape Cod on November 11 and later moved to Plymouth on December 16. Of the 102 passengers aboard the *Mayflower*, only 52 made it through the first winter. The *Mayflower* set sail back to England on April 5, 1621 with only half its crew as others had also succumbed to the deadly New England winter.

By 1627, other congregants joined the group making a total of 160 people living in Plymouth. An influx of new immigrants began in 1630 with the coming of the Puritans. Together the two groups founded Harvard College in 1636 for the purpose of training pastors. They also formed what would be called the Congregational Church, a most influential church in American religious life.

The Pilgrims were not legends, but real people who risked everything for the right of free worship, apart from the authority of the king and state. It is estimated that 35 million Americans trace their ancestry to the 52 Pilgrims who survived the first winter, including five American Presidents. The influence of the Pilgrims on American life is immeasurable.

Thanksgiving: A Distinctly American Holiday

If there is a religious holiday that is truly America, it is Thanksgiving. No matter what one's faith, a pause to give thanks simply makes us better people. This American tradition goes to the credit of the Pilgrims who faced every kind of adversity, but ultimately prevailed in settling a permanent colony in Plymouth after their landing on the *Mayflower* in 1620. Ensuing years saw the Pilgrims and Puritans celebrate the day until 1682, but it was not until the American Revolution that George Washington and the Continental Congress set a nation-wide day of prayer and public thanksgiving *"acknowledging with grateful hearts the many and signal favours of Almighty God."*

It was in 1863 that President Lincoln proclaimed the final Thursday of November to be the official date of Thanksgiving *"in all states,"* a date that held until December 26, 1941, when President Franklin Roosevelt and Congress signed a bill into law making the fourth

Thursday in November a national holiday of Thanksgiving.

There is a common thread in the development of this American holiday, that being giving thanks even in times of adversity. Gratitude has a way of changing our focus from thinking about our trials to thinking about blessings and even if life is difficult, we simply feel better by focusing on the good.

Consider this: The four occasions cited in which this uniquely American holiday developed were all times of trial. The Pilgrims had just endured the worst year of their lives as 48 of their total number of 102 were dead and those left were facing unimaginable hardships of exposure and hunger, and yet they gave thanks. When George Washington proclaimed a nation-wide day of thanksgiving, America had just lost 26,000 patriots in the cause of independence, and yet the infant nation gave thanks. When Lincoln set "an official date for all states" to give thanks, it was a time the nation was engaged in a great civil war. When President Roosevelt signed a bill that the fourth Thursday of November was a national holiday of Thanksgiving, it was only 19 days after Pearl Harbor, the Day of Infamy.

There is a message here for everyone. Gratitude enables us to focus on our blessings and not our losses. It may not change how things are, but it does change who we are.

Reconciling America

Seldom, if ever in our lifetime, has America experienced so much angst over a transition of power as seen in the inauguration of a new president and the retirement of another. With over sixty members of the House boycotting the inauguration, marches of protest in Washington and across the country, celebrities threatening to move to Canada, the polarization of the left and right, and the challenges of the legitimacy of the election questioned, the climate of life in America is on edge. We might say "America is at war," but at war within itself. As our country moves through a difficult transition both of power and ideology, it is time to move forward with reconciliation. Failure to do so will only polarize our country further and impede the progress of being the "greatest nation on earth."

The present election and transition of power is not the first political challenge to America's unity. The election of 1796 was the third quadrennial presidential election, but the first to be contested. John Adams of the Federalist Party ran against Thomas Jefferson of the Democratic-Republican Party. The campaign was an acrimonious one with each party trying to undermine the other. The outcome was that Adams was elected President since he received the most votes and Jefferson the Vice-President. These two great statesmen put their differences aside to work for a better America.

When America came apart during the great Civil War, it appeared there would be two countries: an America comprised of the northern states, and a Confederacy comprised of the southern states. Even church denominations split to northern and southern churches. Thankfully, the union survived and the differences of these former enemies were eventually resolved. In time, most Protestant denominations reunited, seeing the need for reconciliation.

History tends to move with a pendulum motion as the electorate evaluates its values and ideologies. Such pendulum effects have certainly been visible in the last several presidential elections. Lessons on reconciliation can be learned from the founding fathers and America in the post-Civil War era as a polarized nation found its unity once again.

In so many ways America again stands at the crossroads of enmity and bitterness vs reconciliation and unity. A reading of Paul's First Letter to the Corinthians finds a church also at odds over issues that seemed important at the time. He introduces his celebrated Chapter 13 with the words, "I will show you a more excellent way," that being the greatest of all virtues. Reaching across the aisle, across the town, or across the country, can be this "more excellent way." America is a nation founded on the principle of reconciliation. Such is the meaning of a democracy. It is time for reconciliation not only in politics, but in every place of discord and rupture.

Some Gave Some—Some Gave All

Memorial Day has, for many, become defined as the beginning of summer. Sadder still, others do not even know what Memorial Day is all about or why we even have such a day. It is often celebrated with family barbecues, stock car races, and beach outings. Has the meaning of Memorial Day lost its real meaning in all the hoopla?

It was first observed on May 30, 1868, when General John Logan, placed flowers on the graves of Union and Confederate soldiers in Arlington National Cemetery. The first state to recognize it as a holiday was New York in 1873, followed by other northern states. Southern states began to memorialize their fallen dead in the Civil War as early as 1866 when the day was referred to as Decoration Day in which graves of the dead were decorated with flowers. It was not until after World War I that the southern states joined the rest of the nation for a day of remembrance for those who lost their lives while in service of their country.

In his Gettysburg Address, President Lincoln coined two immortal phrases that summarized the meaning of remembering those who gave their all. While dedicating the hallowed ground at Gettysburg, one of his immortal phrases was: *"The world will little note, nor long remember what we say here; while it can never forget what they did here."* Memorial Day is about never forgetting what has been given for the cause of freedom and the stand against tyranny.

The second immortal phrase is: *"the last full measure of devotion."* Simply put, they gave their lives, all they had to give. That is a "full measure" by any standard. That full measure means those who gave it will never see their children grow up, graduate, walk down the aisle in matrimony, experience the joy of being a grandparent, or grow old with one's beloved. So much ends when a soldier draws his last breath in service to his country. So much is given. That full measure can never be forgotten.

Jesus said, *"Greater love has no man than this, that a man lay down his life for his friend."* Those who have laid down their lives for their country have lain down their lives for people they will never know and lain down their lives for a cause, that of life, liberty, and the pursuit of happiness. On Memorial Day, we can indeed, *"never forget what they did in giving their last full measure of devotion."*

Freedom Is Never Free

In his time-honored speech at Gettysburg remembering those who had given their lives on that battlefield, President Abraham Lincoln coined several phrases that define what freedom is truly about. Although his speech predated the first observances of remembering the fallen in the immediate post-Civil War years, (as early as 1866 in the South and 1868 in the North), phrases coined by Lincoln capsulate the meaning of remembering those who made the ultimate sacrifice.

One indelible phrase is: "the last full measure of devotion." How often that phrase is quoted in speeches and prayers of remembrance, and how descriptive of a life given. What greater sacrifice than that of one's life, severing all remaining occasions of enjoyment or momentous moments no one would want to miss. The total deaths of US soldiers in all wars is 1,354,700+. Visit any one of the military cemeteries around the world such as Normandy, Manila, or Belgium, with rows and rows of crosses, and one gets the enormity of that last full measure of devotion. Kneel beside a headstone in silence and think about the young life laid down. Verses from John McCrae's famous poem say it best:

> *We are the dead, short days ago,*
> *We lived, saw dawn, saw sunset glow,*
> *Loved and were loved, and now we lie,*
> *In Flanders fields.*

A second enduring phrase from Lincoln's address is "honored dead." What a suitable description of those who gave that last full measure. These are those who cannot return a smile, receive an embrace, and who have left loved ones behind. These are truly the honored dead.

A third unbounded phrase is "that these dead shall not have died in vain." The fruit of any soldier's sacrifice is the uniqueness of America coined by other such eternal phrases as that of Katherine Lee Bates in beholding "beautiful and spacious skies, amber waves of grain, or purple mountain majesties." Beyond America's beauty is the American ideal of opportunity by developing one's life with gateways of fulfilling dreams. Appreciating America's beauty or pursuing opportunities, or worshipping where one chooses, the right of free speech, the right to assemble, and so much more, ensure the maxim that these dead shall not have died in vain.

Patriotism is loving America and gratitude to those who made and keep her free. Freedom is never free!

Attack Ads and the 9th Commandment

In every election, whether national, state, or local, the media is bombarding the populace with all kinds of political ads. Unfortunately, most of the ads are not about what the particular candidate plans to do if elected, but attacks on the opposing candidate. With each ensuing election, it appears the ads just keep sinking to lower levels. One wonders if any person running for office can really be as bad as the ads portray him/her to be.

Negative campaigning tries to win the advantage by attacking the opponent's personality, opinion, or record, often by distorting the truth or taking things out of context. It's easy to do with editing technology, and often the public is drawn into believing something about a candidate that is far from who the person is or what they stand for. It's the dangerous game of dirty tricks and sometimes can come back to bite the candidate running the ad. For instance, the 2008 US Senate race in North Carolina saw an incumbent senator dub in a voice over her opponent's picture saying, "There is no God!" The voice sounded like that of the opponent, but was not her at all. The opponent actually was a Sunday School teacher and the ad backfired on the incumbent and she lost the election by a nine-point margin (Wikipedia, *Negative Campaigning*).

While the First Amendment grants free speech and freedom of the press, candidates who thrive on destroying their opponents through falsehood and half-truths should be scrutinized for the content of their character. After all, they are violating a higher law than that of the Bill of Rights, that being the Ninth Commandment regarding bearing "false witness against one's neighbor." In determining your vote, why not go with the Ninth Commandment because, after all, honesty trumps everything else.

The Politics of Negativity

When an election is just around the corner, the populace is beset with the campaign styles of every election: negative campaigning, namely candidates making disparaging remarks about their opponent, distorting the facts, taking statements out of context, innuendo, or even political set-ups which candidates hope will boost their own political position. The politics of negativity are apparent in local, state, and national elections. The sad thing about negative campaigning is that they work. People tend to believe what they hear and see in whatever form of media.

Repetitive blasts of negativity create a mindset that a political opponent is as bad as they come. Hearing negativity over and over, however, does not make it true, but sadly does tend to form opinions and when voters step into the ballot box, the politics of negativity often influence voting preferences. Such negative propaganda does have its affect.

We do look up to candidates who are people of faith and are grateful they make their decisions based on their tenets of faith. It is unfortunate that some candidates who present themselves as people of faith also engage in the politics of destruction for the opposition. Such does not go hand in hand with religious conviction. What does go hand in hand are such virtues as honesty and integrity about oneself and one's opponent.

The Bible is forthright in its admonition about honesty towards another. In fact, it is the Ninth Commandment, "Thou shalt not bear false witness against thy neighbor." Accountability for one's actions hold, even in politics. Further, the Apostle Paul asserts that people of faith should "speak the truth in love" (Ephesians 4:15). Simply put: Tell the truth, but tell without the politics of destruction.

Finally, as you cast your vote, consider the politics of negativity, or as Paul said in Philippians 4:8 "Think on these things."

Freedom "From Religion" and the Miniscule Minority

When I read the Guest Commentary written by self-proclaimed atheist/agnostic writer Annie Gaylor, I wondered why a newspaper would devote a full quarter page for this woman to espouse her agnostic views that are frothed with half-truths and innuendo regarding a prayer before a football game at the University of Tennessee. Evidently Ms Gaylor and her watchdog group were concerned one local pastor spoke a sectarian Christian prayer before a football game against the University of Florida. Okay. But before she gets her ire up, she and her Freedom from Religion group should have listened to the response from the chancellor of the university regarding what is allowed in terms of prayers held at the university.

Further, what right does someone from Madison, Wisconsin, have to tell the chancellor and the governing board of the University of Tennessee as to how to run their university? Ms Gaylor alluded to having received "complaints" about a prayer spoken before the Tennessee/Florida game. I have found during the course of my life that when people say, "We are getting complaints," or "People are saying," it is 99% of the time the person making the statement and not some nebulous group of people out there somewhere. If Ms Gaylor is going to say complaints have been received, she should substantiate such a statement with such facts as "who," and "how many."

Thirdly, Ms Gaylor makes the statement that "Up to a quarter of today's college students" identify themselves as non-religious. Throwing out categorical statements without substantive data is just another way to push your own personal agenda. If such statements are going to be used in a commentary, present the unbiased facts based on empirical research. Albeit, college students in this generation generally do not participate in organized religion, just like their parents and grandparents in previous generations. But are one fourth of the students at the University of Tennessee or the University of Florida atheists or agnostic, I seriously doubt it!

Finally, Ms Gaylor alludes to the fact the tax-supported University of Tennessee is home to many foreign students and they might be "offended" by a Christian prayer. Ms Gaylor, you are right. It is a tax-supported university supported by the good people of Tennessee. It is great to have international students at American universities, among them the very best universities on earth, but these students are guests of our country and guests of the universities the tax-paying people of this country built and paid for. I was recently in an Islamic country and when the Muslim cleric climbed the minaret, gave the call for prayer, and all the Muslims fell on their knees facing Mecca, I was not offended, because this was *their* country and I was a guest in their country. But this is *our* country. These students are guests in our country, all here with the privilege of a student visa.

Ms Taylor and her group seeking freedom from religion should be reminded that the colonies were settled by people seeking their right to religious expression. All the men who signed the Declaration of Independence were, in fact, Christians, thirty-two Episcopalians, thirteen Congregationalists, twelve Presbyterian, and so forth. When there was no place to hold worship in Washington, Presidents Jefferson and Madison invited local clergy to hold worship in the House of Representatives, a practice that continued until after the Civil War.

America is a country of fairness in every way, far more than any other country on earth. Great efforts are made to give ear and voice to everyone, majority or minority. But it is time for the trend of the minuscule minority's ability to determine the course taken for the overwhelming majority to cease, as in the case of Ms Gaylor's Freedom from Religion group.

Les C. Wicker

Why Shouldn't Students Say "God Bless America!"

On December 30, 2015, the school board attorney for the Hadden Heights, New Jersey school district received a letter from ACLU attorney Edward Barocas that the practice of Glenview Elementary, a school within the district, was violating the Constitution by the daily ritual of beginning the day with students saying, "God bless America" after their pledge to the American flag, a ritual related to 9/11 first responders.

When local reporters questioned Barocas whether there had been parental complaints about the practice, he said he had received none. Simply stated: There will be no more "God bless America" at Glenview Elementary. A lengthy and costly court battle with the American Civil Liberties Union would usurp much needed funds intended for education. Similar battles in other school districts have been costly and schools need their funds for instruction, not costly court battles.

The message seems loud and clear that there is a quiet, insidious transition of values in America. While little note is taken of such incidents as banning "God bless America" in Haddon Heights schools, such occurrences transpire with increasing frequency across America. It all affects who we are as a people.

When events such as the Haddon Heights school district occur, those making the challenge usually make reference to the Founding Fathers or the First Amendment. Who were these men and what did they believe about religion?

All of those who signed the Declaration of Independence were men of faith, but intelligent enough not to impose their faith on anyone else as is evidenced in the First Amendment. The amendment states: "Congress shall make no law respecting an establishment of religion or prohibiting the free exercise thereof." It is a stretch from a law that Congress might impose regarding the establishment of a religion to such challenges as that of banning children from saying "God bless America."

What is implied in the terms "God bless America" or "In God We Trust" or "One Nation Under God?"

Normally, most people assume it is the Judeo-Christian God of the Old and New Testaments. While the Judeo-Christian understanding of God is subliminally implied, the truth is America is a multicultural nation of multiple religions, yet all of whom reference a higher power as "God," or as Thomas Jefferson stated in the Declaration of Independence, "Creator."

The term "God" is a much broader and more inclusive term than those who blur the distinction with the claim it is pushing one religion over another. In truth, it's an affirmation of America's belief in a higher power versus a complete void. The underlying truth is a definition of who we see ourselves to be as a people.

The use of such terms as "God" implies such moral traits as goodness, love, hope, and kindness. Forbidding the use of such terms creates a society void of such feelings and people become hard and even sinister. Just reference the Soviet Union experience under Lenin and Stalin who promoted a society void of religion.

While the assault against any expression of religion has been focused primarily in public schools, one wonders where the foothold will lead. Schools are vulnerable and soft targets. But by incrementally subduing one school district after another, the challengers will become more emboldened, ready to take on larger challenges, including removing "In God We Trust" from the currency and "one nation under God" from the Pledge of Allegiance. While this seems far-fetched, it is not as far-fetched as it might sound.

> It is ironic that every president normally ends his speech of importance with "God bless America," but suspect for elementary school children to utter the term.

> It is ironic that all patriotic hymns, including the national anthem, reference God is some

way, but any reference to his blessing is unconstitutional.

It is ironic that the sculpture of Moses and the Ten Commandments are carved on the Supreme Court building, but any allusion to God violates separation of church and state.

It is ironic that the original constitutions of all states mention God, but it violates the Constitution to use the term in a public school.

It is ironic that all U.S currency has emblazoned on it the words, "In God We Trust," but a school district allowing children to ask his blessings will find the school board in a court of law.

The gateway is what it has always been for people. Americans are good people, ones who weigh thoughts of what is right and what is wrong. They will be pushed so far, then they push back. Such will be the case of such nonsense as no more "God bless America" at Haddon Heights and the countless other such cases that surface out of the blue.

Just wait and see!

The Prince of Peace and the Angst of the Day

There have indeed been worse times than those we are experiences today, but has there been a time with so much angst of people against one another as witnessed in our present-day state of affairs? Polarization, discord, and strife seem to be the order of the day. The prevalence of angst has become so ordinary, it is almost as if it is expected, just another story to be reported in the news. Regardless of the magnitude of the particular expression of angst, it is taken in stride, knowing that yet another fracas is just around the corner. Sad! Yes, it is really sad because every incident affects someone's life, and the sum total of our common humanity, driving us further apart from one another.

We are all too familiar with those polarizing expressions usually affixed to a political party, media, gender, ethnic group, or platform of expression. It is epidemic! It's the right vs. the left; harassment and "me-too moments" vs. "I didn't do it;" taking the knee vs. boycotting a sport; The Dream Act (DACA) vs. deportation, open borders vs. building walls; core values vs. progressives; statues vs. legacy; unbiased news vs. fake news; snowflakes vs. time-honored; collusion vs. transparency; Millennials vs. Baby Boomers; "resistance" vs. embracement; political correctness vs. conventional; black lives matter vs. blue lives matter...and on and on it goes.

The above points of angst surface in dramatic and painful ways such as was witnessed in the mass shootings in Sutherland Springs, Texas, the Las Vegas Music Festival, and the Pulse Night Club. They further emerge at encounters between protesters and counter-protesters at such points of conflict as the University of Virginia and numerous other flash points.

Add to the above, threats like ISIS, Kim Jong Un, the Russians, or the Chinese. It's a scary and contentious world at home and abroad. But has the world not always been a world of violence, war, disarray, and madness? Is it any different now than when God entered the world in Bethlehem 2000 plus years ago? Israel was occupied by Rome and Israel hated its invaders. There was an "establishment" both in government and religion. Life was cheap. It was a world filled with angst.

Into this chaotic, hate-filled world comes the "Prince of Peace." The message of the angels to the shepherds was, "Glory to God in the highest and on earth peace and good will among men." In the angst of this world today, that message of peace and good will among people still holds. Is it an oversimplification to believe that the Prince of Peace can indeed bring peace to a world like ours?

A More Excellent Way

Is America being polarized, yet again, by racial issues of black and white? Who among us would want to return to the '60's when the watchword was *"Burn, Baby, Burn!"* The trauma from seeing entire blocks of the Watts neighborhood of Los Angeles, California, burn was dreadful. There were thirty-four deaths and 4,000 National Guardsmen called out to quell the disturbance. The thought of it sent a chill down the spine of every American. It was the nation's worst racial incident until that of Rodney King in 1991. King was stopped for drunk driving, whereupon, he was beaten by four policemen, an event that happened to be videotaped. The outcome of the Rodney King event was that fifty-five people were killed and 2,000 injured.

None of us would want to return to those horrid days! The recent events of the shootings of Alton Sterling in Baton Rouge and Philando Castile in St. Paul and the aftermath of the deaths of five innocent policemen in Dallas, indicate we may be headed back to those days. There are no words for the sorrow and pain, frustration and anger, these horrendous events have set in motion. That, coupled with the pain and anguish of Ferguson and Charleston have given race relations in our country a set-back no one expected. Data from the Pew Research Center, published in June, 2016, found racial tensions are clearly on the rise. Comparing both blacks and whites, the survey showed only 34% of African-Americans thought race relations were good, compared with 59% in 2009, with a similar drop in the white population from 66% in 2009, to 46% at present. Escalating and polarizing is clearly not the direction we need to go. To the contrary, we need to be reaching out to one another.

It would be difficult for white people to fully comprehend the feeling of racial profiling, for being suspect simply because a person is a person of color. Truly, Black Lives Matter. At the same time, White Lives Matter. Indeed, all lives matter. In the hours after the Dallas ambush, stunned civic leaders pleaded for citizens to repair the rips of the nation's social fabric. David Brown, the African-American police chief of Dallas, said, "Our profession is hurting. We are heartbroken." At the memorial service for the fallen officers, Rev. Bryan Carter echoed Chief Brown, saying, "We refuse to hate each other. We commit ourselves to pray together."

After reviewing all the things that polarized the Corinthian community, the Apostle Paul, prefaced his celebrated 13th Chapter with these words: "I will show you a more excellent way." Of course, that more excellent way is love, what we most desperately need in our country today.

Overwhelmed by Sadness

The tragic events on Valentine's Day, 2018, at Marjorie Stoneman Douglas High School in Parkland, Florida, are startling, and bring a sense of sadness to the heart and soul that words cannot describe. While it is not unlike other school shootings in recent times, perhaps its occurrence so close to home intensifies the emotions of disbelief and sorrow. It could have been one of the high schools of Collier County, or any community across America, just as well. But it doesn't matter where it happened to occur, the loss and pain are just the same...bewilderment, emptiness, grief that will not go away, parents and spouses who lose what is most precious in their lives, and a that sense of finality that the loved one will never be seen again. Beyond the pain of grief, the young and innocent lives that were snuffed out, with all the hopes and dreams that dwelt in each heart: the life that was ahead, and living each day with love and joy...all gone!

Many churches across America had services of remembrance for the young people and adults whose lives ended so tragically and suddenly. At our church, pictures of the students and teachers were put on the power point screen as names were called and roses placed on the altar in memory of each life lost. I had personally prepared the power point and the brief bio of each victim. In the preparation, seeing the faces of these beautiful young people and dedicated teachers was harrowing. The kids were all so beautiful, so innocent, and their very countenance spoke of lives of happiness and joy, and plans for their future. The teachers, some of whom took the bullets to protect the kids, were good, good people who had dedicated themselves to the young lives under their care, and who were always there for the kids.

When the Second Amendment was put into the Bill of Rights, that is the right to bear arms, the arms that were available were muzzleloaders used for hunting. Having just fought the British and threats from Indians on the frontier gave every reason for the framers of the Constitution to ensure the right to bear arms. Muzzle loading guns were the most advanced weapon of the day. Could the founding fathers have conceived the assault weaponry of today? Could they have imagined an event like that experienced in Parkland and the horrific, unspeakable pain accompanying such a loss? It is a stretch from a muzzleloader to an AR-15.

While we are overwhelmed with sadness with tragic events like Parkland and while we have utmost sympathy for the pain of loved ones who have lost what is most precious in their lives, the slaughter goes on. We know that Jesus feels the pain, but beyond that, what would He advise our country in terms of the shootings and the loving care of our children?

Appropriate Racial Identification

Every racial or ethnic group has a preferred name by which they wish to be identified. Honoring that request by identifying them by their preferred label is not only important, it is the right thing to do. Who wants to be misidentified or identified by an inappropriate or archaic label? No one.

All racial groups have labels by which they wish to be identified. It only takes a little thought to correctly identify the preferred label and using it will gain respect for the user and give respect to the identified group. Euro-Americans think very little about their correct racial identification and casually refer to themselves by the color code of "white." Correct labeling is not so much an issue when you are in the majority and your racial label is taken for granted. However, such is not the case for minorities.

Every minority has experienced transitions of preferred labels. While it now sounds "Uncle Tom" to refer to African Americans as "colored," which was once the preferred term and is still retained by the NAACP. The Black Power movement of the sixties and seventies sought to instill racial pride in the race by transitioning the preferred name to "black." Such phrases as "Black is beautiful" were promoted in African American communities to reinforce pride in being black and to transition the label to black. The preferred label today is African American. Such a trend may also be found in the preferred label of Native Americans as the correct identification has changed from American Indian to Native American. Immigrants from Asia prefer to be called Asian Americans and those from south of the border prefer the term, Hispanic Americans.

Mislabeling someone's race or ethnic group can be an insult. Correctly identifying someone's racial or ethnic group takes little effort and is a sign of respect. Why not show the respect that is due!

The War on Christmas

Is there really a "War on Christmas" or is it just paranoia? If there is a war on Christmas, whence is its source? Other than agnostics and atheists, there is no one out to do Christmas in, but the subliminal messages the Politically Correct Policemen (PCP) keep sending indicates there certainly is an undercurrent against this sacred holiday for Christian believers. While this genre of political correctness is invading our culture, the invasion appears innocuous, that is, we just don't think about it, and in fact, unknowingly jump on the PCP bandwagon.

Cases in point: "Merry Christmas" vs "Happy Holidays." Now is December 25 about "Happy Holidays" or is it about the birth of Christ. Obvious answer! It is not about "Happy Holidays" or "Winter Break," it's about Christmas and there is no getting around that. But we don't want to offend anyone. That would just be a political bummer. So we acquiesce to the changing culture.

But who is offended? No one is offended by wishing Jewish people a Happy Hanukkah or Happy Kwanzaa for those African Americans who wish to celebrate their feast of gift giving. People of the Jewish and Christian faith have co-existed for two centuries and never found offense in wishing one another joy during their special holiday.

The PCP's have indeed invaded both the culture and marketplace. Just look around at the shopping malls and count the stores that advertise the season with "Merry Christmas" as opposed to those who inoculate the season with "Happy Holidays" or "Season's Greetings." Or get a cup of coffee once served in a bright red cup with Christmas themes that is now only a "bright red cup." Or look over the selection of cards available to send to loved ones and friends and consider how many say "Merry Christmas" vs how many simply say "Happy Holidays." Or check out the wreaths available for your front door—do they say "Merry Christmas" or "Happy Holidays?"

You see, my friend, the holy season we call Christmas is under attack. December 25 is Christmas. There is no getting around the meaning of the day. Let's push back with a very "Merry Christmas!"

CHAPTER 4

The Colors of Holidays and Seasons

Saint Valentine's Day

Yes, there really was a Saint Valentine, but the one for whom the day is named was a martyr and the day was placed on the church calendar to honor his martyrdom more than any ascription to love and romance. One legend, compiled by J.C. Cooper, in The Dictionary of Christianity, states that Saint Valentine was a "priest of Rome who was imprisoned for succoring persecuted Christians." While contemporary records of his assisting believers were destroyed, a compilation of Bede's *Martyrology*, states that Saint Valentine was persecuted as a Christian and interrogated by the Roman Emperor Claudius II.

During the interrogation Claudius was so impressed by the priest, he tried to convert him to Roman paganism in order to divert an execution. Valentine, in his devotion, attempted to convert the emperor to become a believer. Unfortunately and to the dismay of the emperor, he had to order the execution of Valentine. However, before his execution, Valentine is reported to have performed the miracle of healing the jailor's daughter, Julia, from her blindness, along with forty-four members of the jailer's household.

The jailer and all of his household became believers. On the evening before his execution, he wrote the jailer's daughter, who was no longer blind, and signed it "Your Valentine." The saying stuck and over the centuries those who deeply care for others adopted the saying, "From your Valentine." It is said that Julia herself planted a pink-blossomed almond tree near his grave. Hence, the almond tree remains the symbol of love and friendship.

Today, Valentine's Day is celebrated around the world, and is, in fact, an official "feast day" in a number of communions of the church. From the final words of Saint Valentine to Julia, "Your Valentine," it has assimilated historical and cultural icons which flavor the day as a time to remember those we love. These include: Red Roses, the favorite flower of Venus, the Roman goddess of love; Cupid, from Roman mythology, the god of desire, affection, and erotic love; and the Heart, possibly originating from the now-extinct North African plant, silphium, a plant that looked like a heart and a symbol of love.

While Valentine's Day has become a big business with over $18 Billion in sales, second only to Christmas, it is a day to remember those we love, and as St. Paul so spoke in I Corinthians 13, "The greatest of these (virtues) is love."

The Silent Spring No More, But Who Is Listening

Remember Rachel Carson and her provocative book, *Silent Spring,* published in 1962, that challenged the chemical industry of the detrimental effects of indiscriminate use of pesticides, particularly on birds? Her research and alarming book awakened conservationists and eventually spurred the reversal of the national pesticide policy, banning the use of DDT. Thankfully, the birds now are still singing.

The problem is so few of us are listening to their melodies. They sing all the time, but do we ever stop to hear the music they are singing? Is it that we have selective hearing and only tune into those sounds that we choose to hear?

No doubt around your home there is a Mockingbird that has claimed your yard as his territory. Before you awaken in the morning, he is already up welcoming in the day with his variety of tunes. There seems to be no end to his repertoire. When he seems to have exhausted his last version of sounds, he just comes up with another bar and keeps on singing. It's almost as if he is your special bird, a gift given especially for you, Hear him out. He is doing his best to awaken you with joy and the sounds of heaven.

A chirping Cardinal is an attention getter for those who enjoy special sounds. When the red bird pipes up his vocal cords, be sure to look to the top of the near-by tree. There you will find the maestro of bird sounds, conducting the sounds of nature. Note: As the maestro, he will always be on his pedestal at the top of the tree.

Every bird has its peculiar song and is recognizable by its call: The Bob White, Sparrow, Purple Martin, Red-winged Blackbird, and so many more. Like any orchestra that blends its sounds into a symphony, nature's orchestra is comprised of a variety of sounds, but when blended is truly magnificent.

Jesus must have had an ear for the symphony; otherwise he would not have mentioned the bird kingdom so often. We are fortunate there is no "silent spring." Enjoy the music! "He who has ears to hear, let him hear." Matthew 13:9.

The Four Facets of Mother's Day

Mother's Day is celebrated in more than forty-six countries around the world. Its origin dates back to the ancient Greeks and Romans, and to England who celebrated a "Mothering Sunday." Credit for establishing Mother's Day in America is given to Anna Jarvis who was born in Webster, West Virginia, where her birthplace is a national shrine. Very devoted to her mother, Ann Marie Jarvis, Anna held a memorial day for her mother in Grafton, West Virginia, on May 12, 1907, just two years after her mother's death. With an intense campaign to recognize mothers, Anna appealed to Congress and on May 8, 1914, President Wilson signed a declaration making the second Sunday of May the official day for Mother's Day.

I personally like the thought of Mother's Day and remember that as a child I would go out in the fields to pick little flowers we called bluettes and give them to mom and she would make a big deal over it. While Mother's Day has come understandably under scrutiny and is even painful for some, let us look at how this day is regarded with affection and with pain.

First of all, everyone has a mother. The day is really about recognizing the woman who brought us into the world and nurtured us along the way. Whether we are young or elderly, we can honor this woman for her years of love, labor, and prayers.

Secondly, every woman cannot be a mother. Some women long for the joy of motherhood, but for various reasons such as infertility or even marital status, are unable to fulfill that longing. We need to be sensitive to these women for whom this day may bring a sense of pain and emptiness as more fortunate women who have the honor of motherhood are lifted up.

Thirdly, some mothers have passed away. Holidays and birthdays, while times of joy and celebration, can also be times of great pain when loved ones who have touched our lives are no longer around. This is especially true of Mother's Day when our mother has been the best of the best, but is no longer around for us to tell her we love her. For these people Mother's Day can be the saddest day of the year.

Fourth, there are mothers whose children are alienated. Sadly, we live in a world where people do not live happily ever after and in some families, for whatever reason, parents and children become estranged. Here the hurt of Mother's Day cuts to the core. What a sad feeling for such a special day!

Let us be grateful to this special woman who brought us into this world and who loved us through the years. Let us also be sensitive to how this day may affect others for whom this day may bring a sense of pain.

Ten Commandments for Father's Day

Father's Day has been around since the early part of the Twentieth Century as a complement to Mother's Day. While Father's Day is less expressive than Mother's Day, it is nevertheless a very important day. What makes a good father? Here are Ten Commandments that every father might consider:

I.   Thou shalt take time with your children.

No one can overestimate the importance of time spent with children. It sends the right message that children are important. The implicit message raises the self-esteem of children simply by an unspoken message that they are valued.

II. Thou shalt play with your children.

While the proverb, "The family that prays together stays together is true," a change of wording from "pray" to "play" is also true. Families who separate recreation to "adult" and "children" commit the fatal error of separating opportunities of connectedness. Parental play with children is but another way of building a children's self-worth.

III. Thou shalt pray with your children.

Family prayer, whether saying grace at meals or family devotions, recognizes the spiritual dimension of life.

Prayer not only builds character, but enables children to build their lives around a love for God and family.

IV. Thou shalt enjoy your children.

Children grow up quickly. One day they are taking their first step, the next it seems, they are going to school; then before you know it they are grown. Make the most of every day while there is time.

V. Thou shalt talk to your children.

We live in this unbelievable world of communication with the internet, text messaging, and cell phones. Unfortunately, most parents spend only minutes a day talking with their children. It is a good practice to have a "talk time" every day. Perhaps this can happen during the family dinner.

VI. Thou shalt know your children's friends.

As children grow, friends take on different dimensions in a child's life. When children are young, it is important to include their friends in family events. As children mature, the influence of friends is paramount in terms of the influence friends may have on a child's life. Such influence can lead a child in a right or wrong direction.

VII.   Thou shalt express love for your children.

Parents can never assume their children know they love them. There are countless ways to show love, but none beats the simple expression of verbally telling the child s/he is loved.

VIII.   Thou shalt build character in your children.

Dorothy Law Nolte's noted poem, "Children Learn What They Live," says it all about character. Simply put, children develop the kind of character they have experienced in their home and by the example of their parents.

IX. Thou shalt encourage your children.

No one has more influence over a child's life than his parents. Encouragement enables a child to believe in himself. It creates positive vibes. Those positive feelings become springboards for success.

X. Thou shalt set a good example.

Children absorb what they see in their parents. The poem, "I'd Rather See a Sermon Than to Hear One Any Day," by Edgar A. Guest, says it all. It's not what is said, but what is visibly done that makes the difference.

Memorial Day: Truly a Religious Holiday

While many view Memorial Day simply as the onset of summer, it is far more than purely a day of ushering in the vacation season. Religious communities do not count it as a "religious holiday," yet it is religious for the many reasons for which it stands: remembrance, honor, respect, gratitude. And indeed, to quote Jesus, *"Greater love has no man than this, that a man lay down his life for his friends,"* John 15:13. The fact is 407,300 American soldiers laid down their lives in the fight against tyranny, aggression, and oppression in WWII alone, not to speak of other wars including the "first down payment" of 26,000 who died in the American Revolution. To gloss over these sacrifices would be a travesty.

It is important that religious communities recognize and pay respect to this day of remembrance for those who in Lincoln's terms made the "last full measure of devotion." Failure to do so would overlook the very privilege given in the First Amendment, that being the "free exercise of religion," a privilege won and safeguarded by those who made the ultimate sacrifice.

Passing on to the next generation the honor and respect due those who have served our country is imperative. The words of President Washington still ring true, *"A primary object should be the education of our youth in the science of government. What duty is more pressing than communicating it to those who are to be the future guardians of the liberties of the county?"* Indeed, President Reagan alleged *"Freedom is never more than one generation away from extinction. We do not pass it on in the bloodstream. It must be handed on or one day we will spend our sunset years telling our children and our children's children what it was once like in the United States where men were free."*

We can be particularly grateful that in Southwest Florida there are such organizations as "The Naples Spirit of '45," to connect the greatest generation with the newest generation. On the upcoming Memorial Day weekend, we can be grateful not only to those who have served our country and made the ultimate sacrifice, but to those who honor the fallen with the many events that memorize and give gratitude to those who have served this great nation. Given all the holiday means, it is indeed a religious holiday.

Labor Day Is Far More Than the End of Summer

Who thinks about Labor Day in terms of its original intent, that being the celebration of labor, anymore? Is labor, one's contribution to the greater good through one's work, whether through sweat and toil or in the high tech spheres of Silicon Valley and the like, the focus of Labor Day? After all, labor is work in whatever form. As such, it must be appreciated for what it is, one's gift of skills and talents for the community of humanity. Nowadays, the meaning of the day has shifted to simply the end of summer or "one last fling" of vacation.

Labor Day is one among ten federal holidays, those being: New Year's, Martin Luther King, Jr.'s, Presidents', Memorial, Independence, Labor, Columbus, Veterans, Thanksgiving, and Christmas. In 1870 Congress created federal holidays to correspond with those of various states. These included New Year's, Independence, Thanksgiving, and Christmas Day. By the late 19th century, as the labor movements grew, trade unionists chose a variety of days to celebrate labor. Labor Day became an official federal holiday in 1894 in the aftermath of the death of workers during the Pullman Strike. As such, it became one of the earliest of federal holidays.

Some federal holidays have been established and later abandoned. A case in point is Victory Day, established by Congress in 1948 to celebrate the victory over Japan and the ending of WWII, only to be abandoned as a federal holiday in 1975. With the shift in the labor industry from predominantly blue collar, the shrinking jobs as technology advances, automation, and buyouts of workers, one wonders if Labor Day will also become an abandoned holiday, or as a study of American adults in 2012 found that 52% thought of Labor Day as only the "ending of summer?" (Wikipedia).

A better approach would be to expand the thought of labor to a much broader and inclusive spectrum. Our labor is ultimately our work in whatever form. It can come in any shape or form. It is a sense of who we are, how we identity ourselves, our sense of fulfillment.

Biblically speaking, work has great value. The very thought of creation was not only that God worked to create the world and all that was in the world, but that God had a sense of fulfillment in what he had labored to do. "He saw that it was good!" Therein lies the joy of one's work, having a sense of satisfaction when a job is done. This sense of satisfaction translates into every endeavor of work. It's just knowing you did a good job and can feel good about it.

Psalm 104 is a celebration of God's work in creation. It is complete adulation in praise of God's work. The Psalmist relates in verse 31, "...may the Lord rejoice in his works." One's work, and the satisfaction therein, is indeed a pale reflection of God's own joy in creation.

Labor Day is more than the end of summer. It is more than a federal holiday. It is a celebration of who we are, our self-worth, and the satisfaction of knowing our lives count through our life's work.

World Communion Sunday—A Paradigm for Faith Communities

We live in a divided world, a world that is becoming more polarized with the passing days. We speak of East—West, Christian—Muslim—Jew, and even as we speak, there is that underlying feeling of nervous tension. It shouldn't be this way. It cannot, in fact, continue to be this way. The world cannot afford the tension as such tension only escalates the walls of division. The fact is the world is getting smaller and has been shrinking in size for some time. It is a time for reaching across the aisle and around the world. The focus needs to be on our commonality and not on our differences.

World Communion Sunday is the first Sunday of October. It is a Sunday in which most all churches celebrate the sacrament of Holy Communion and it has become one of the most venerated of special Sundays. There are, of course, churches that celebrate the sacrament at each gathering as it is the focal point of weekly worship or at mass. Some Protestant communions celebrate the sacrament weekly, and others at regularly appointed times. Through World Communion Sunday the sacrament has become a point of Christian unity for the faithful on this given Sunday.

World Communion Sunday originated with the Presbyterian Church (USA) in 1936, but soon spread to a number of other communions. In 1940 the National Council of Churches led its extension to churches throughout the world.

World Communion Sunday, originally called World Wide Communion Sunday, has taken on new relevancy and meaning in a world where global division and terrorism have undermined peace and unity, and fear divides the peoples of God's earth. On this day we celebrate the oneness of Christ in a world in need of peacemaking. The sacrament underscores our oneness, rather than our differences, and the numbers of church communions participating in World Communion Sunday keep growing, now including a wide spectrum of the faith.

Could World Communion Sunday and the unity it brings believers around the globe not serve as a paradigm for other needs in our world, that we are One earth, One people, One race, One humanity, One body, One family, One?

Why I Love Thanksgiving

Holidays are special times in our lives. Normally, such days are celebrated with family and friends, even if it means long distance travel. These are, in fact, times we remember the things of greatest importance: family, faith, and freedom. Thanksgiving, a distinctively American holiday, encompasses all three in a most distinct way.

Great effort is made to be with the most important people in our lives, that of family. It happens generation after generation, that families rally around each other and an especially prepared meal to give thanks. As a child, my family would go to our grandparents on Thanksgiving. As parents, we made the trek to our parents, spending the noon meal at one set and the dinner meal at the other. As grandparents, having the children and grandchildren in, warms the heart that this special day of gratitude is a centerpiece for a family gathering once a year. The importance of the family, that we have one another, and that we are able to enjoy these treasured moments is worth everything.

Thanksgiving is a time of faith. From the days of the pilgrims, it is a reflection of God's good gifts, even in times of adversity. One might say, it's a focus on the positive, remembering that God is good and the life God has given is a blessing. It would be difficult for a family to gather around a table laden with food without a prayer of gratitude, or even the thought of God's goodness. Even in times when families are facing challenges or losses, the emphasis on gratitude can ease the pain. Perhaps that is why the Apostle Paul wrote to the Thessalonians "Give thanks in all circumstances."

The third focus of this holiday is freedom. Separating this holiday from a thought about the privilege of living in America would be next to impossible. While the pilgrims faced the trials of life in this new land, they understood that even in the face of hardship, there was something special about this new land, that it would be a land of opportunity. By any measure, America is the greatest nation on earth, and, yes, there is "something special about this land.," from sea to shining sea.

Thanksgiving: It's really about family, faith, and freedom.

The "Get Ready" People

An occasional street preacher would pass through the town in which I grew up. These men were marginalized by established religion. They held no degrees, no endorsements, no credentials, no judicatory ordinations. They were just called to preach. They were all itinerant—no pulpit of their own, no office, no staff, no one to report to—kind of "what you see is what you get" personalities. By and large, they were shabbily dressed, but spoke authentically what they felt led to say. Their message was one of repentance and preparation. They often warned their listeners to "Get ready to meet Jesus."

There lived another "Get Ready" man who lived quite some time ago. He lived in the wilderness and also came preaching a message of repentance and preparation. His name was John the Baptizer. He was dressed in camel's hair and had a leather belt around his loin. He, too, was marginalized to the established religion of the Pharisees, Sadducees, and scribes. No doubt, they just wished he would go away.

Think of it:

> They had degrees, endorsements, credentials—he just had himself.

> They wore ecclesiastical garments—he wore camel's hair.

They slept in rabbi's quarters—he slept under the stars.

They were polished—he was coarse.

They had the smell of frankincense—he had the smell of camel dung.

They ate at the king's table—he ate wild honey and locusts.

Yet, when the time came for his baptism, Jesus chose John, this itinerant prophet, to be his pastor. There has to be a message here! After all, Jesus said: "The meek shall inherit the earth."

Advent is the "Get Ready" season. John was right for who is worthy even to untie the shoelaces of the One who came to be baptized by John in the River Jordan. John's message, like all the "Get Ready" men is a call to repentance and preparation. And, yes, God calls us all to examine our lives, but no matter how unworthy we may feel, just as He loved John just the way he was, He loves us just the way we are, and He transforms us into something more. The Word is made flesh: Get Ready!

Santa Vs Jesus

Perhaps you have heard about the latest board game, out just in time for Christmas. It is called "Santa vs Jesus," and was created by the London based company,

Komo Games. It is played by two teams, each of whom represents one of the Christmas personalities, Jesus or Santa. The challenge of the game is to see who wins the most "believers."

The creators of the game, Julian Miller and David McGranaghan, thought the game would be a hit like other games such as "Exploding Kittens," or "Cards Against Humanity." They reasoned that for years people have wondered who ruled Christmas, "Santa or Jesus." While the game has four stars on Amazon, any serious-minded person would question trivializing the sanctity of the central figure of Christian belief in a board game that pits him against a legendary figure of Western culture known as Santa or Saint Nicholas. The two are not the same and equating the two creates a mindset they are both fictional characters.

Santa Claus, as this figure in known in America, is also known as Saint Nicholas, Kris Kringle, and Father Christmas in European cultures. The legend grew out of traditions surrounding the fourth-century Greek bishop and gift giver to the poor. The personas of this legendary saint found expression in various German, Dutch, and British cultural traditions as this most benevolent saint came to visit children and the poor on Christmas.

The image of Santa became Americanized by the poem, "The Night Before Christmas," by Clement Moore, written in 1823. It was in this classic poem that Santa became dressed in a red suit, had is sleigh pulled by reindeer, and was able to mysteriously come down a chimney. The image was enlarged by the artwork of Haddon Sundblom beginning in 1931 with his creations of Santa for the Coca-Cola Company.

Needless to say, Santa, while he represents benevolence and good will, in no way can be compared to Jesus who is a part of the Godhead. He is "The Word made flesh," "the Eternal One." At the very heart of Christmas is God's Son, entering humanity. Making light of his eternal glory in a game pitting him against Santa Claus sends the wrong message. Sadly, however, in our commercial world in all its politically correct venues, Santa may be winning. Albeit, a Santa can be placed anywhere, but it's against the law to place a manger in public place.

Final Thoughts

While the book is a kaleidoscope about certain areas of life, faith community, patriotism and country, and certain holidays that need attention and focus, one must understand that life itself is a kaleidoscope. The passing of time is like rotating the cell with the cause and effect of changing designs and colors. A second principle of the kaleidoscope is the principle of multiple reflections. Such is life.

Life is a progression into the future. It is always moving and changing as new opportunities and issues surface. The joy of life is to turn the cylinder and not only to see the colors, but to be engaged at focal points which enrich one's life and the lives of others. It is the people who do not just observe the colors, but become those who create the colors that change their world. Those who sit and do nothing will never change their own lives and will have no impact on the world in which they live.

The challenge is to be a "Border Buster," in your world. Be who you were created to be. Make a difference! Know that when you leave this world, it will be a better world because you have passed this way.

Turn the kaleidoscope canister. Love the colors of life!

About the Author

Rev. Les Wicker grew up in North Carolina. After graduating from Greensboro College, he received a Master of Divinity degree from the Divinity School of Duke University. He later went on to child development and family relations studies at the University of North Carolina at Greens-boro where he received a PhD. He has served churches in North Carolina, Wisconsin, and Florida. He and his wife, Phyllis, have two sons, Robin and Dale, who along with their families live in Florida and North Carolina.

Dr. Wicker has received a number of recognitions for church growth in North Carolina, Wisconsin, and Florida. He received the Distinguished Public Service Award from the Board of County Commissioners of Catawba County, Newton, North Carolina for outstanding community work.

Dr. Wicker is the author of *Preparing Couples for Marriage, The Fundraising Guidebook for Benefit Golf Tour-*

naments, and *The Miracle Church.* He has led numerous seminars on self-esteem and personal growth, and growing the church through marketing outreach.

Made in the USA
Columbia, SC
15 October 2018